D1127782

MARCH/HOLMBERG
LTM   1987

Traditional
Bhutanese   Textiles

White Orchid Books

Barbara S. Adams

TRADITIONAL
BHUTANESE TEXTILES

White Orchid Press
Bangkok 1984

Published by White Orchid Press,
487/42 Soi Wattanasilp, Pratunam, Bangkok, Thailand.
Printed by Craftsman Press, Bangkok.

TABLE OF CONTENTS

PREFACE

This preliminary study of the traditional textiles of Bhutan was indirectly inspired by Her Majesty the Queen Mother of Bhutan, who graciously presented to me the first Bhutanese weavings I had ever encountered, during a brief but delightful meeting in Hongkong with Her Majesty and her sister Tashila many years ago. I hung the textiles on the walls of my house in Kathmandu, marvelled at their beauty, and had to wait ten long years to see anything even vaguely similar.

Unexpectedly, about five years ago, similar weavings began to appear in the shops at the Buddhist Stupa at Bodhnath near Kathmandu. They were trickling in on the backs of Bhutanese pilgrims who had come to Kathmandu for a big *wang* — meaning prayer meeting — to be given by a high Lama or Buddhist priest. The *wang* was delayed for two months as the Lama fell ill, and the pilgrims began to sell a few of their cloths to finance their extra stay in Kathmandu. Nowadays they come to trade their old and often unwashed cloth, some of which have been worn by as many as four generations, for Chinese brocades and Indian polyesters.

I have never visited Bhutan, although I hope that some day good fortune will allow me to do research on the weaving in that beautiful country. My entire collection was hence acquired bit by bit in Kathmandu, where I have lived for the past twenty-two years. Like most collectors, I initially just intended to buy a few more pieces — to cover a bed, or hang on an empty wall — but then each foray to Bodhnath yielded another discovery, a yet unnoticed design, another tantalizing hint of techniques and rituals which I had to try to understand: in short, I was hooked!

A good sampling of my collection of Bhutanese textiles is illustrated in this book, which is the result of a four-year quest for nearly non-existent information and documentation about a weaving culture which deserves a place in the artistic history of the world. I hope the visual impact of these beautiful weavings will compensate for the many inaccuracies and gaps in the text. Hopefully, this is a first step towards a comprehensive and definitive exposition by the Bhutanese themselves of their great weavings and weaving traditions.

I would like to humbly thank Her Majesty the Queen Mother of Bhutan, whose generous gift so many years ago sparked the interest in Bhutanese weavings which resulted in this book.

David Barker, photographer and friend, devoted patience, time, and loving care to photographing my collection. Given the complexities and eccentricities of each piece of fabric, and the limited facilities available in Kathmandu, his was truly a marathon task, which he executed with enthusiasm and sensitivity.

Thanks are also due to David Herbert, art dealer and friend, who introduced me and Bhutanese tapestries to the museum and gallery world of New York; to Mr. Numeroff and Maureen Zarember who courageously lent their New York Galleries for exhibitions of Bhutanese fabrics at a time when they were still unknown; to Peter and Alexandra Rose who introduced the tapestries to designers as far away as Saudi Arabia.

Much gratitude goes to Alan Wardwell and Maureen Aung Twin of the Asia Society New York, and to Patricia Fiske and Mattiebelle Gittinger of the Textile Museum, Washington, all of whom encouraged and reinforced my conviction that traditional Bhutanese textiles deserved to be seen, studied and appreciated.

In Kathmandu, Deki and Yeshe of Thamel and Sushil Lama of Bodnath patiently helped and encouraged me to acquire the best. Thanks also to Barbara Brennan for arranging lectures and exhibitions of Bhutanese textiles for the international community in Kathmandu, and to Gordon Temple, Carlton Coon and Desmond Doig for providing photographs from Bhutan.

Thanks also goes to H.K. Kuløy, who actually made this book happen. His professionalism and straight-foward approach, and his skillful editing, have turned an amateur's dream into a useful reality.

The unsung heroes of this book are the weavers, past and present, of the Kingdom of Bhutan. Perhaps the only real thanks I can give them is this book. Their works of art have gladdened and enriched my life. I hope this modest work expresses my gratitude.

Note: A number of the textiles illustrated in this book were shown at the exhibition "The Textile Art of Bhutan", March 10th to April 6th 1984, at the J. Camp Gallery, 380, West Broadway (Soho), New York.

CHAPTER I

GENERAL INTRODUCTION

The tiny, isolated Himalayan Kingdom of Bhutan has perhaps the last surviving weaving, or cloth-based culture in the world. Closed to most outsiders until very recently, Bhutan has jealously guarded its cultural integrity of which weaving is an inseparable part. Bhutan has produced, and in some instances continues to produce, a range of most interesting and beautiful textiles. These fabrics, which until recent years were largely unknown to all but a few intrepid travellers and explorers, are now beginning to appear in a few private collections and museums outside Bhutan.

The first exhibition of Bhutanese textiles that I am aware of, was mounted in 1958 at the Crafts Museum in New York, by Jack Lenore Larson, the United States' leading textile designer. The fabrics were lent and presented by the Queen of Bhutan. There is also a small museum in Neuchatel, Switzerland, which has a collection of Bhutanese textiles, presented by the late King, on condition it be kept on permanent exhibition. In fact, until recently, the only Bhutanese textiles to reach the outside world, were gifts from the Royal Family or high officials to prominent visitors travelling through Bhutan.

Although fabric was, and probably still is, as important in the overall culture of Bhutan as it was in South America in Pre-Columbian times or is in Indonesia, very little has been written about it. One can only hope that this preliminary review will stimulate an extensive and profound examination of a unique weaving culture and what it has produced.

Early glimpses of this cloth culture are provided by travellers such as Samuel Turner, who observed in his book "An Account of an Embassy to the Court of the Teshoo Lama in Tibet" first published in 1800:

"An inferior on approaching a superior, presents the white scarf and when dismissed, has one thrown over his neck, with the ends hanging down in front. Equals exchange scarves on meeting, bending towards each other with an inclination of the body. No intercourse whatever takes place without the intervention of a scarf; it always accompanies every letter, being enclosed in the same packet, however distant the place to which it is dispatched. . . . ."

"Punakha Dzong", drawn by William Daniell, ca. 1830.

More than one hundred years later, J. Claude White in his book "Sikkim and Bhutan", describing a ceremony involving one of the Rulers in Bhutan, writes:

"Now began an almost interminable procession of lamas, officials and retainees, each bringing a scarf and presents, till the Penlop was almost smothered in scarves, while the whole nave, from end to end gradually became filled up with heaps of tea, bags of rice and India corn, fabrics — silk, woolen and cotton — of all colors and values with little bags of gold dust and rupees appearing on the top."

He then went on to describe how each individual retainee:

"Dumped their presents with a bang on the floor and whipped out their scarves to their full length. . ."

The expression "the fabric of society" really comes into its own when applied to Bhutan. Every nuance of wealth, status and rank, as well as all human interchange was and to a large extent still is regulated by an unwritten set of rules relating to fabric. Even today, scarves must be worn for all official and religious occasions, their color and quality defining rank and function. Gifts to and from the noble families were traditionally pieces of cloth — given in uneven numbers of from one to seven depending on the rank of the receiver. In former times, a man's wealth was measured by the number of *kho*, also known as *boku*, which he owned. He would sometimes wear one over the other in ostentatious display. Equally, a woman's wealth was measured by the number of *kira*, or dress pieces she owned, and the quality and complexity of the weaving in those *kira*. Handwoven cloths are still required to be worn in

the *dzong*, huge fortresses still used as religious and secular administrative centres, and in the presence of important officials. The color and characteristics of these cloths also depend on an unwritten set of rules and rituals of politesse.

In his chapter on arts and industries in Bhutan, White writes:

"Every house of any importance has large workrooms attached, in which weaving is carried on, and the stuffs produced, consisting of silks for the chief's dress, woolen and cotton goods are excellent; and a good deal of embroidery is also done."

The traditional centers of weaving were and still are in Eastern Bhutan, in places like Kurtey, Tashigang and Bumthang. Weaving is, however, still also a part-time occupation all over Bhutan. Army officer's wives while away the time when their husbands are away on duty; hired weavers weave cloths for noble households; peasants weave for their basic household needs. Some estimate that well over half of the about one million population of Bhutan is engaged during some part of the year in weaving! Certainly White's observation is as true in 1983 as it was in 1905.

Bhutan also produces extraordinary appliqués and needle embroideries and combinations of the two. These are often pictorial depictions of religious themes, local deities, etc., which are hung in the palaces and *dzong*. These range from smallish works, bordered and hung like painted *thankas,* or temple banner pieces; covering large outer walls of temples. These huge religious hangings have been seen by very few foreigners, since they are carefully unrolled and hung only for special religious occasions, and then carefully

Celebration in a Bhutanese *dzong* with huge *thanka* on the wall.

stored away again. Other smaller, simpler appliquéd articles were used for altar cloths, saddle blankets, seats for lamas or high ecclesiastical officials, and probably many other purposes. To have an idea of the splendor of these hangings we refer again to the observant Mr. White, describing the Durbar Hall at Punaka:

'The center, or nave, was hung with a canopy of beautifully embroidered Chinese silk. Between the pillars were suspended chenzi and gyantsen hangings of brilliantly coloured silks — and behind the Tongse Penlops seat, a fine specimen of kathang or needlework picture, a form of embroidery in which the Bhutanese excell and which compare favourably with anything I have seen in other parts of the world."

The embroidered and appliquéd temple hangings which White describes in the Punaka *dzong*, are of rarely equalled beauty and excellency of execution, but similar works can also be found in China, Tibet and in Mongolia in the excellent museum at Ulan Bator. Hence, in this limited work the choice

has been made to concentrate on the most unique of Bhutan's textiles: "loom embroideries".

THE LOOM

Most weaving in Bhutan is still done on a very basic type of sling-back or back-strap loom, which is easily transportable and can be attached to any fixed surface such as a wall or a tree. The weaver sits on the ground or floor, leans back against a wide leather strap which holds the threads taut, and deftly manoeuvers a dizzying number of seemingly extraneous threads into the background cloth as it is being woven: thus is produced the infinitely varied embroidery-like designs which can be seen on both ritual and utilitarian textiles all over Bhutan.

This continuous and discontinuous supplementary weft (sometimes called floating weft) technique, has been developed into a unique and sophisticated art in Bhutan. It is most often employed to produce the three heavily embellished and matching strips of cloth, about eight feet long and a foot and a half wide, which when sewn together become the *kira*, or woman's dress piece.

THE KIRA

The *kira* is a rectangular piece of cloth about 125 cm. x 205 cm (5' by 8') which is held at the shoulders by silver clips *(coma)* and belted with a *kera* to hold a deep front pleat in place. This type of dress was already being worn in 1905 according to White. Referring to Sir Ugyen's daughters, he writes:

"Guard House near Tassisudon", drawn by William Daniell,
ca. 1830.

Women dancers wearing their finest *kira*.

Group of Bhutanese, the women wearing *racchu* scarfs and the man a white *kupney* scarf.

" . . . .all wore the pretty and distinctive dress which consist of a long piece of Bhutanese cloth, woven in coloured stripes, draped around the figure and fastened on the shoulders and confined at the waist by a band of brighter Bhutanese cloth."

Mrs. Blanche Olschak, during her trip to Bhutan in 1971, writes of this dress

"Their dresses follow the finest folk tradition, each being a hand-woven masterpiece; every valley has its own colorful pattern, the flower ornaments of the East being especially esteemed. Every woman's dress, the most precious being woven of Bhutanese silk in double-sided patterns has a secret. It is neither cut nor sewn. Worn over a silk long sleeved blouse, it consists of a 'sheet' of three long strips, each strip being an elbow length wide and four els long, an old ell being about 21 1/2 inches. This beautifully woven 'sheet' has to be most carefully pleated and draped around the body. At the shoulders it is held together by silver buckles which are connected by a chain ornament with lucky golden symbols. These buckles replace the old time fibulas which are now rarely seen, all being collectors pieces. The long dress is held together around the waist with a long woven sash of matching colors and at least a foot wide."

One finds roughly three types of *kira:*

(a) The striped cloth with a double-sided design, is used for everyday wear, in contrast to the categories below which are woven for special or ceremonial occasions, and usually worn by the upper classes in Bhutan. Tashigang is famous for its striped silk, double-faced loom — embroideries, of which there are many types, each given a special name.

(b) *Kira* embellished on a coloured background and decorated with similar materials and designs as the kushutara. These are called *Naushem* (blue background) and *Jangshem* (green background).

(c) The *kushutara,* considered the most aristocratic *kira,* is always embellished on a white backgound. It is usually of hand-spun, hand-woven Bhutanese cotton, decorated in various colors and designs, usually with raw silk *(buré),* but sometimes with wool or cotton thread. The rarest and often the finest, are embellished with refined or filiment silk, revered by the Bhutanese as *sechu.*

Traditional greeting with scarf.

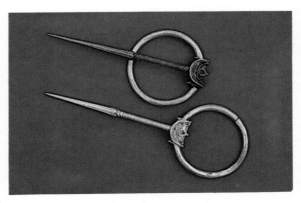

Antique *fibulas* used previously to fasten the *kira* at the shoulders.

All the fine, old *kushitara* are said to have been woven in Kurtey.

The older *kira,* and some still woven in obscure villages, are embellished with vegetable-dyed thread, usually with freer, "spacier" designs than those woven today. Often Buddhist symbols are more obvious and graphic than in the more recent pieces, where the work becomes increasingly more dense and complicated, and the Budhist influences tend to disappear into the overall pattern. These antique *kira* have often been handed down for generations and can be in poor shape by the time they reach the museum or collector. They have been worn and used in hard cold climates and are often darkened by smoke, food, and other more or less identifiable stains. They do, however, respond well to love and pure soap, and with each washing the incredible virtuosity of the woven designs, and the vibrant classic vegetable blues and reds, become more assertive and pleasing to the eye.

In more recent years, an acid, aniline pink has come into fashion, and still more recently, the use of synthetic lurex thread. Yet the inherent aesthetic sophistication of the weavers turns these jarring elements into a pleasing, rather than garish, final product.

THE KOH

The *koh* is a man's garment similar to the Tibetan *chuba,* except that unlike the *chuba* it is always worn tightly belted, with a narrow belt *(kera),* so that the upper portion forms a sort of loose pouch or pocket into which a number of objects including a pet Lhasa Apso can be safely transported. The *koh* is worn knee-length, over cotton white shirt *(tegu)* whose cuffs and collar are turned back to show touches of white at the wrists and neck. A small knife or dagger is usually carried in the pouch, and often a longer one is attached at the waist to a belt and worn outside the *kho.*

Tashigang has been the center for producing the double-faced, richly embellished striped cloth most traditionally used for *koh* as well as for a certain special type of

Clips, *coma*, used in more recent time for the fastening of the kira: The *coma* with dragons has its original chain.

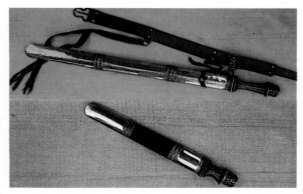

Ceremonial sword with gold decoration, worn with the *koh* for important functions. This particular *patang* was a gift of the late King of Bhutan to Mr. Gordon Temple.

Ceremonial silver dagger which is worn inside the pouch of the *koh* which is formed by belting tightly with the *kera*.

kira. Koh are usually made from three strips of hand-woven cloth about 9' long and 1½ feet wide. Traditionally an extra strip 9 feet long and 10 to 12 inches wide was added to the "*koh* set".

As with the *kira*, the most revered *koh* are of silk, both *sechu* and *buré*. Other traditional materials for *koh* are an unembellished checked raw silk, also woven in the Northeast, and a checked, woolen, almost Western type of cloth, usually woven in Bumthang. When made up, the *koh* is lined with cotton or a subdued Bhutanese raw silk, sometimes with touches of soft refined silk or Chinese brocade at the neck and cuffs. In olden days the *koh* was worn over colorful, wool embroidered boots with soft leather soles *(palhum)*, but today, practical leather shoes and knee-length socks seem to have taken over.

The *koh* is truly a national dress in Bhutan, worn by every single Bhutanese male, from the King to the humblest of his subjects. Thus, the *koh* is a symbol of the homogeneous and egalitarian nature of this unique society.

THE KERA

The *kera*, or *chhudang* as this belt is called in Eastern Bhutan where it is woven, is similar to the *pangkep* (see below) in feeling and type of weaving, but without the center diamond, the side borders, or the boldness of design. They are woven strips of cloth about 30 cm (12 inches) wide and 122 to 183 cm (4—6 feet) long, and are usually fringed only at one end. Two pieces are usually woven at one time and cut apart at the central less embellished portion which is hidden when the belt is worn. This long cloth is folded thrice, wrapped tightly around the waist, and held in place with the fringed end, which is tucked into the top of the belt. Today they are only worn in villages and by the older generation. The younger generation of Bhutanese prefers the narrow bright modern belts which cinch the waist in the Western manner, to the bulkier but more beautiful *chhudang*.

THE KISHUNG

The least known, but perhaps the ethnographically most interesting of the textiles to be found in Bhutan, are the *kishung*. A kind of dress or poncho, the *kishung* was woven in remote and inaccessible villages in the Kurtey area of East Bhutan. Unfortunately, information about this unusual woven and embellished dress is also obscure and inaccessible. Bhutanese from Thimpu and Paro are unaware of their existance and maintain that they are not from Bhutan. Bhutanese from Eastern villages state that they are taken out of trunks and worn for special occasions, but often give conflictig reports about their history and their ritual significance. Some say that they are brought out only every two years for certain mysterious rites, perhaps related to the pre-Buddhist Bonpo religion. There are whisperings that the occasions for which they are worn involve various forms of magic. . .Certainly the most beautiful *kishung* are embellished almost entirely with Buddhist symbols.

The *kishung* was woven in two richly and finely embellished panels, which were then joined, leaving space for the head and arms. The 10.25 to 20.5 cm (4—8 inches) bottom border was woven with an intricate carpet-like technique which the Bhutanese from Kurtey area say cannot be reproduced today.

Unfortunately these antique ponchos remain a fascinating mystery, but since there are probably no more than two or three hundred of them left in the world, they deserve to be treated with the reverence accorded an endangered species, and properly researched and catalogued.

THE CHAKSEY PANGKEP

Less "showy" than the heavily embellished *kira*, but equally beautiful to the conoisseur's eye, are the cloths generally known as *chaksey pangkep*. These are long, fairly narrow, kelim-like woven cloths heavily fringed and bordered with narrow strips sometimes embellished with Buddhist symbols. *Chak* means hand; *sey* means wash; *pang* means lap and *kep* means cloth. Interpreting literally, they are cloths for washing hands and covering the lap. One might say they were a type of serving cloth, used in the homes of noble families. These *chaksey pangkep* vary in length from 8 to 14 feet and in width from 2 to 4 feet, depending on their function. Such long, usually vegetable-colored cloths, which are seldom seen in modern Bhutan, seem to divide roughly into three different categories, according to subtle differences in size, pattern and function.

(a) The *chaksey pangkep* is the most intricate version of this cloth. Apart from serving sometimes as a lap cloth it was also used to cover the arm while serving the nobility, and as a towel for them to wipe their hands on after eating. A specially fine one is sometimes folded for an honored guest to sit on, or hung on a wall. Usually a large central elongated diamond design indicates the importance of the person using it.

(b) The *pangkep* is considered the most ordinary of the three categories and was mostly used for covering the laps of the upper classes while they were eating. It is usually narrower than the other categories, and the embellishment less intricate. Often the side borders are totally unadorned. According to my Bhutanese sources, the *pangkep* is smaller and has less work and a less impressive central diamond design than the *chaksey pengkep,* but otherwise it is similar.

(c) The *chukep* or *dongkep.* The Bhutanese say that there is a larger, slightly different version of the *chaksey pangkep,* called *chukep,* which was folded in half and worn as a sort of an apron as a sign of respect by a Bhutanese citizen when approaching the King or a high official. As recounted by one of my Bhutanese sources it was not exactly worn, but rather held on from behind by a retainer, perhaps to symbolically separate the common man from the important official he faced.

All three of the cloths just described as *chaksey pangkep* were usually and traditionally white with vegetable blue and red *buré* embellishment. There are some glorious exceptions. Perhaps the most rare and beautiful of these incorporate a softly colored raw silk or silk design on a dark red raw silk background. This soft but vibrant red, seen in most of Bhutans really antique textiles, is lac dye, also indigenous to Bhutan and called *jatsho,* and is the most revered colour in the Bhutanese spectrum. To explain how this dye is produced in Bhutan, it seems convenient to refer again to Mr. White:

"There is a great deal of stick lac grown in the valley of Tashigang but the Bhutanese do not carry on its culture in any systematic manner which seems a great pity, as if placed under proper supervision the industry might have a great future before it. Its culture is unusual. Lac is an insect growth, and is cultivated on two distinct plants. Small pieces of lac containing colonies of the insect are placed on the stem of a shrub called GYATSO-BUKSHING in the autumn, and this plant is regularly cultivated and planted in fields on the hill sides. In the spring these growths, which have meanwhile spread a few inches over the stem of the plant, are cut off and placed on the branches of a tree called GYATO-SHING. On the trees, during the summer it spreads rapidly over all the branches, and the crop is gathered in the autumn. With the present want of system, there are no plantations for the purpose and the cultivator has to depend on any trees he may find growing wild in the jungles."[8]

It seems that these insect growths are then ground and pounded and somehow treated (accompanied by many rituals and taboos) to become the famous *jatsho* dye, but an in-depth exploration of the dyes and dying processes in Bhutan are beyond the scope of this study. It would take many months and perhaps years with the weavers of Bhutan to really master this and other subjects related to cloth production.

It is my intention here just to hint at the variety and complexity of these textiles and the culture which produces them. Obviously a comprehensive and satisfactory explanation of the real uses and meanings of these cloths will have to wait until the Bhutanese themselves begin to examine and write more extensively about their own culture and history.

YATA

Yata cloth is hand-spun, hand-woven wool, embellished in mostly geometric designs with heavy woolen patterns woven with a border and joined it becomes a carpet, called *dengkep.* Three strips joined become blanket or bed-cover called *charkep,* used in olden days as a shawl or raincoat, which protected against the high altitude cold of Bumthang. The older pieces were made from wool from Tibet and Bhutan. Nowadays much of the wool is imported from New Zealand. This wool is much softer, but lacks the insulating natural oils of local wool used in the old days. Since Bhutan does not have the carpet weaving tradition of the Tibetans, these *yata* pieces often served the functions that Tibetan rugs would. Today it is fashioned into the short, typically Bhutanese jackets which are often worn over the *kira* in cold weather.

CEREMONIAL SCARVES

Aside from the already mentioned Bhutanese textiles, there are many other subtly varying utilitarian and ceremonial weavings. Perhaps the most fascinating, in relation to custom and usage, are the ceremonial scarves.

Scarves worn by the women of Bhutan are called *racchu*. About 6 ½' long and about 11/2' wide, the *racchu* is worn folded and draped over one shoulder, and is only brought about both shoulders when entering the dzong or for other ceremonial occassions. When paying respects to a Lama it is unfolded and worn loose around the shoulders.

The *racchu* is usually in various festive shades of red, maroon or orange, and is embellished at the fringed ends with very fine loom embroidery. The *ada racchu*, rarely seen today, was worn by women in Eastern Bhutan and was embellished all over, the designs somewhat resembling the center strip of the *chaksey pangkep*. The *racchu* were traditionally woven in silk or raw silk with silk or raw silk embellishment. Today they

Officials assembled in front of *dzong*.

are often rayon on a rayon mix.

Scarves worn by men are called *kupney* and are much larger than those worn by women; usually about 10' long and 4' wide. The color of the scarf depends on the rank of the man wearing it. For example, a commoner without official rank wears a white scarf, of cotton or raw silk. Assistant District Administrators and village leaders wear red scarves with white stripes; high civil and religious officials and High Court Judges wear maroon or red, and Ministers and

Village couple dressed for their daily work in the fields.

a letter was always wrapped in a scarf, so they had selected the whitest of scarves without a spot, to envelop the letter to His Excellency, and hoped that its purity would be considered an emblem of their own perfect purity of mind and intention"![9]

Deputy Ministers wear orange. Aside from the King, only the Je Kempo, the spiritual head of Bhutan, wears a saffron color scarf, thus denoting his religious authority.

The *kupney* are intricately draped and wrapped about the shoulders so that they can be ceremonially "unfurled" for the traditional respectful bow to the King or the Je Kempo and sometimes other high officials.

Smaller white silk scarves are exchanged in greeting among ranking officials, and are offered to high Lamas as a sign of respect. Letters and presents are often wrapped in scarves and deities are draped in scarves to show reverence and respect. In short, scarves represent the infinite variety of rite and ritual still inherent in the Bhutanese culture, and only a person born into that culture can fully understand their meaning, and the subtlety and grace with which they are used.

There is a lovely example of this subtlety and grace, again in White, speaking of his diplomatic mission in Bhutan:

"The Thimbu Jongpen, acting as spokesman, made a pretty little speech, saying that as according to the Bhutanese custom

The sketchiness and possible inaccuracies of this preliminary study of perhaps the world's last living weaving culture are evident, and one hopes the Government of the Kingdom of Bhutan, and its weavers, will take over where this book leaves off, and provide us with the information and historical and cultural insight which collectors and admirers lack. The best of the Bhutanese textiles can hold their own anywhere in the world as genuine works of art. Even the humblest have an irresistable directness and charm. My mind jumps to a young man who attended my first exhibition of Bhutanese textiles in New York. He asked if he could film the textiles in the show. Surprised I asked: "Why film?" "I am a dancer", he said, "and the rythms in the designs of these tapestries are so inspiring that I'd like to build a choreography around them." I dream of some day wandering through the halls of some great museum and seeing the walls come alive with the rhythms of the old Bhutanese weavers. Sooner or later their moment of glory will come.

We let Mr. White have the last word:

"Possibly the excellence of the work produced in Bhutan owes much to the feudal system which still prevails there. Each Penlop and Jongpen has his own workmen amongst his retainers, men who are not paid by the piece, and are not obliged wither to work up to time or to work if the spirit is not in them, and consequently they put their souls into what they do, with the result that some pieces of splendid individuality and excellent finish are still made. No two pieces are ever quite alike, and each workman leaves his impress on his work."

Men performing traditional harvest dance.

CHAPTER II

THE *KIRA*

A. VARIOUS STRIPED, DOUBLE-FACED WEAVINGS

1. Well executed cotton embellishment in Buddhist primary colours on a mixed rayon and cotton background. This style is called *aikapur* when the brocading is in yellow and/ or white. 212 cm x 165 cm. (All measurements exclude the fringes). This piece is called Dromchu Chim because it is embellished in four different colors.

2. Detail of plate 1.

18

3. An antique *menta* with red and black raw silk embellishment on heavy hand-spun Bhutanese cotton. A double-faced striped piece in called a *menta* when white predominates in the stripes between the embroidered areas. 220x162.

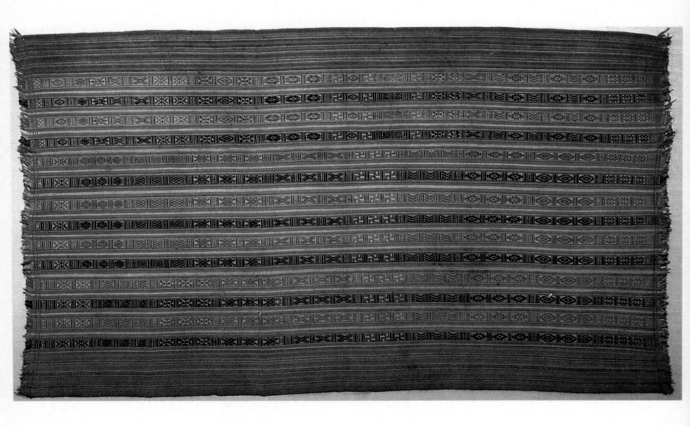

4. A portion of the *menta* showing stripes and embroidered areas.

5. A typical *lungsema* from the Tashigang area in silk on raw silk, in soft reds and greens. 250 cm x 135 cm

6. A section of the fringe area.

7. *Sechu* (filament silk) with green and red *sechu* enbellishment on yellow stripes interspersed with floating weft technique on wider blue stripe. 220 x 128

8. A detail of the front.

9. A detail from the reverse side.

10. This type of yellow and red stripe is loved by the Bhutanese and is known as *mentse mata:* Yellow *sechu* embellishment on *sechu* red with turquoise touches. 252 x 130.

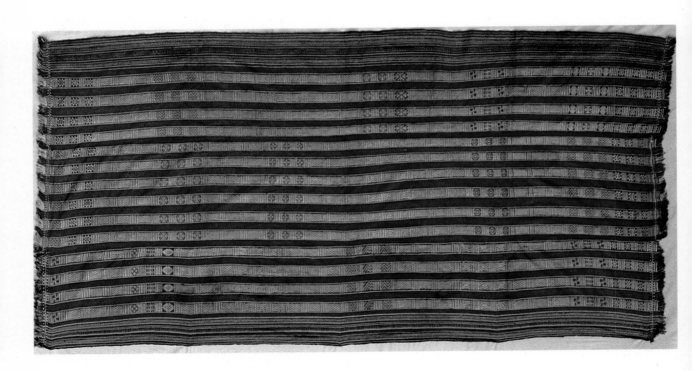

11. A detail illustrating the border and fine design of *sechu* embellishment.

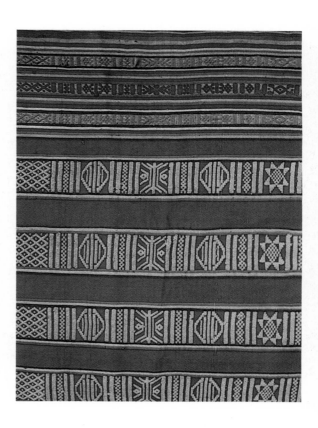

12. *Jhadi Chim*.   A beautiful old striped *sechu kira*.   The fringed ends are finished with tiny embroidered swastikas.   265 x 137.

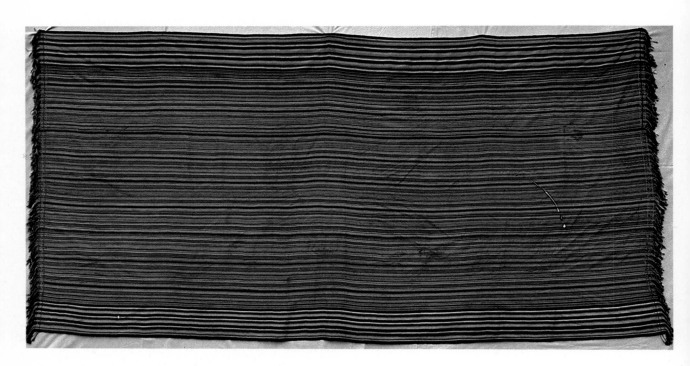

13. An enlarged portion of the swastika design at the fringed end.

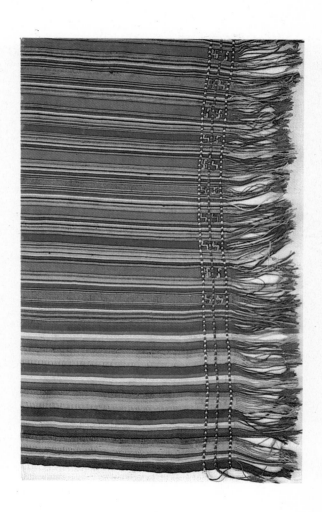

B. *JANGSHEM*

14. An unusually large and finely executed contemporary *jangshem*, evidence of continuing excellence of Bhutanese weaving: Touches of lurex thread is very modern as is the busy decoration on the striped borders. 257 x 157.

15. The unusual embellishment on the striped border is shown in greater detail.

16. Detail of a faded *jangshem* which originally was probably similar in colour to plate 14. This is a perfect example of how aniline colors fade, with the help of the sun and modern detergents. Full size 225 x 120.

C.   *NAUSHEM*

17. A recent, but slightly damaged *naushem* with an unusual design giving a mountain or cloud effect. 240 x 135.

18. This detail shows a closer view of the unusual design.

19. *Naushem;* very light cotton, probably Indian with wool embellishment. A pleasing regular design on greyish blue faded background. 50 to 60 years old. 230 x 127.

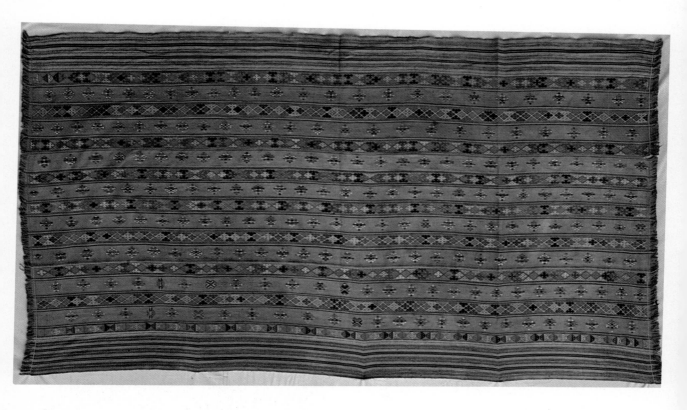

20. Detail

21. Detail of the reverse side showing the unfinished character of the newer kiras.

D. *KUSHUTARA*

22. A cotton *kushutara* with aniline raw silk embellishment. Classic kira, 20 to 40 years old. 235 x 135.

23. Detail of plate 22 showing complex end border designs. This portion of the *kira* forms the back portion of the dress when worn.

24. Elegant *kushitara* of heavy Bhutanese cotton with bold raw silk design incorporating unusual greens and mauves. Small, charmingly worked Buddhist symbols on strip next to the striped border. 50 to 70 years old. 225 x 142.

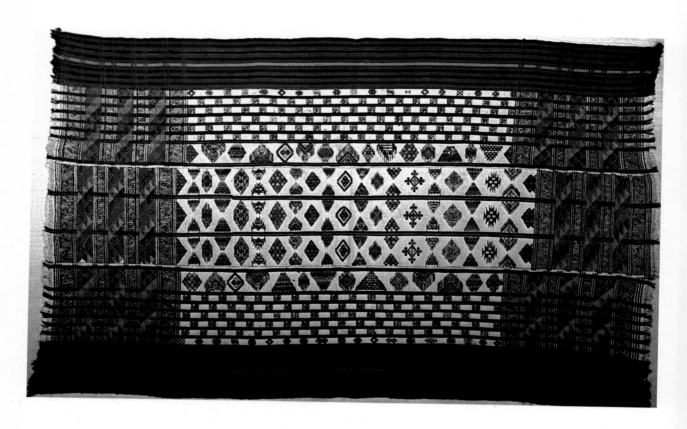

25. Heavy Bhutanese cotton *kushutara* with unusual green in the *bure* brocading. Elegantly embellished white center portion. 230 x 142.

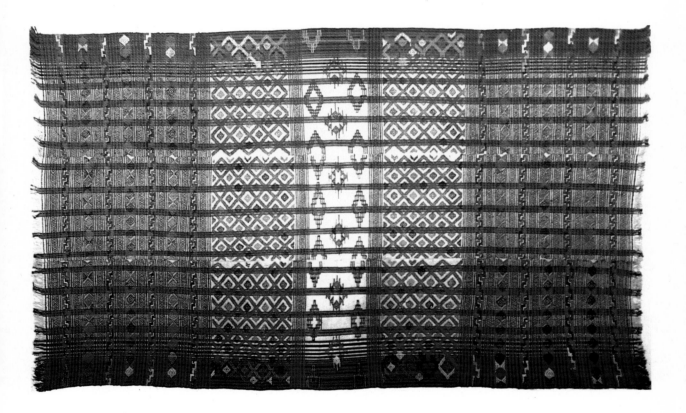

26. Antique *Kushutara*. Mainly vegetable dyed raw silk decoration with raw silk striped borders. Sparse raw silk adornment with sweep of empty portions creating a pleasing sense of movement. Striped raw silk border. Probably 19th century. 275 x 122.

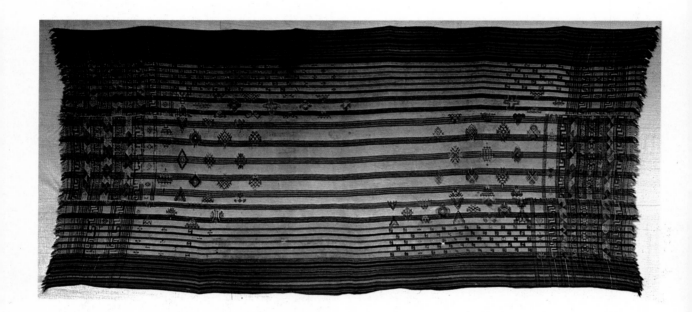

27. Detail of the border design.

28. Soft vegetable dyed *buré* embellishment on a warm cream background with a "spacy" design. May have been woven by the same weaver as number 26. Probably 19th century. 265 x 132.

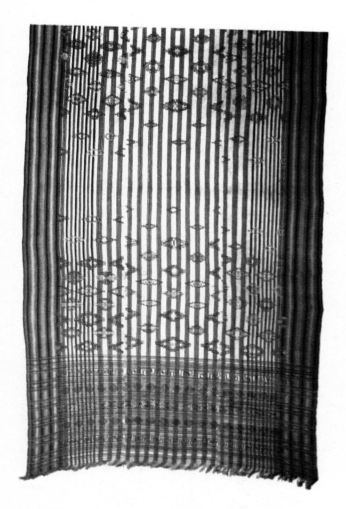

29. The interesting *buré* embellishment of the center panel.

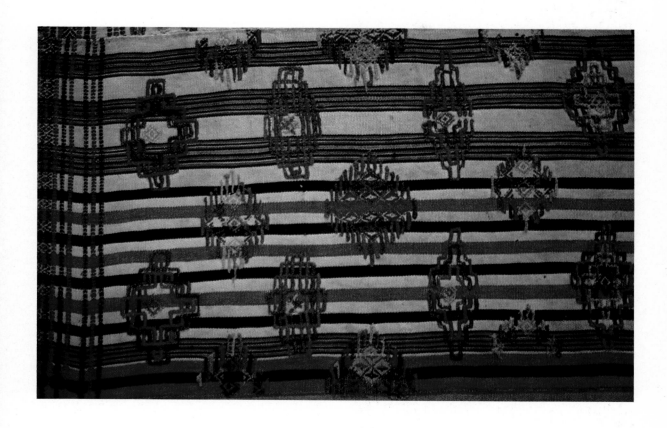

30. Classic, simple, old *neringma kushutara,* with yellow and white *sechu* embellishment on the striped borders. The large empty space in the center disappears into a wide front pleat when worn as a *kira.* Probably 19th century. 225 x 122.

31. Close view of the *sechu* embellishment.

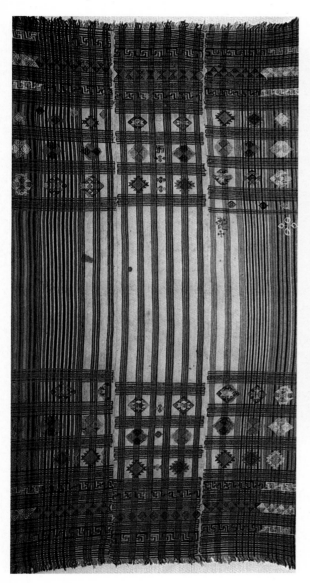

32. Coarse, unsophisticated *kushutara,* with touches of wite and yellow *bure* on the border. 60 to 80 years old. 270 x 135.

33. Detail of work on striped border.

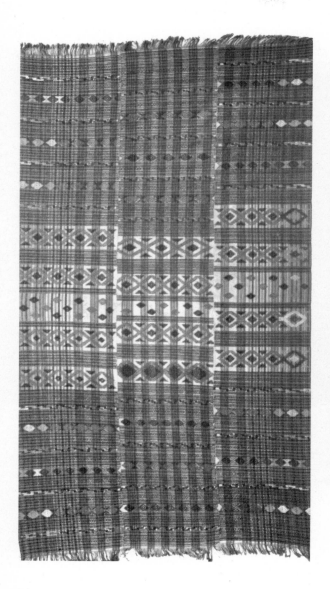

34. Similar in design to number 32 except that this piece is much older according to the quality of the colour. Interesting brocading on the striped side borders. Probably 19th century. 235 x 125.

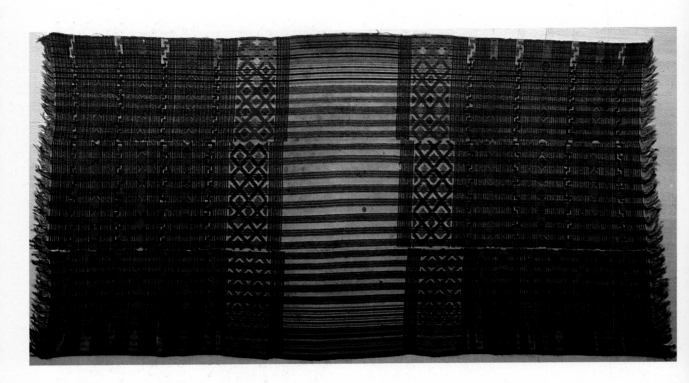

35. Design on end border. 36. Detail of carpet-like design near centre.

37. Bulky, peasanty—feeling *kushutara* with bold bright blue and red brocading and interesting touches of yellow. Lovely striping. 255 x 147.

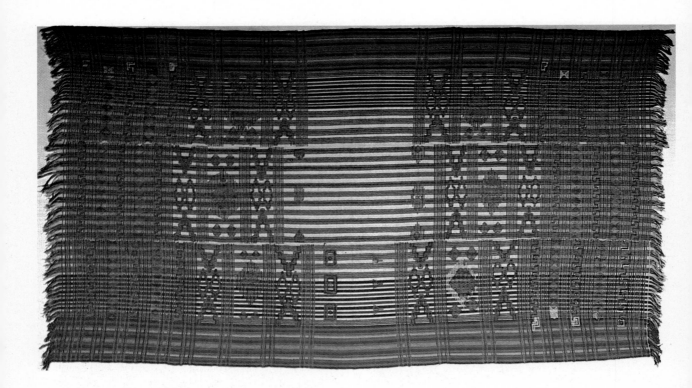

38. The unexpected use of yellow is seen in this side border detail.

39. This view of the reverse side illustrates the absence of threads, a sign of meticulous workmanship.

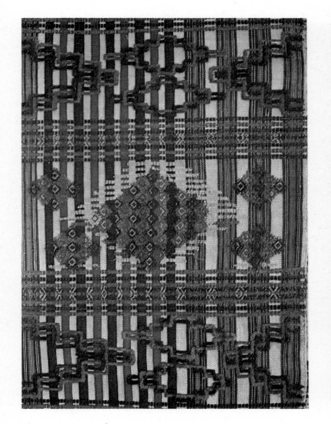

40. The interesting use of the unusual green in the stripe, and white embellishment on border provides a pleasing effect. 265 x 135.

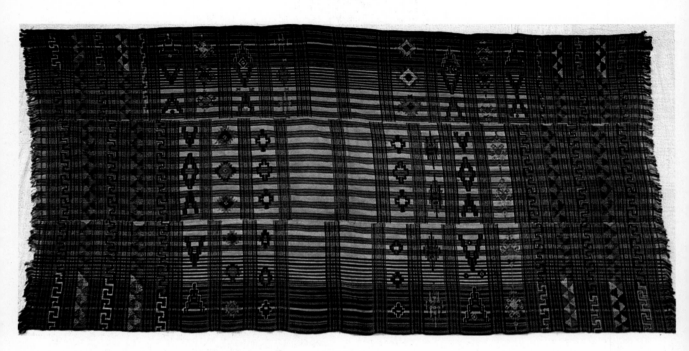

41. Detail of the striking use of white to bring out border design.

42. *Kushutara:* Dark red and blue *bure,* free floating designs with touches of yellow and green. The graphic Buddhist symbols bounce engagingly off the striped inner border. 60 to 70 years old. 270 x 135.

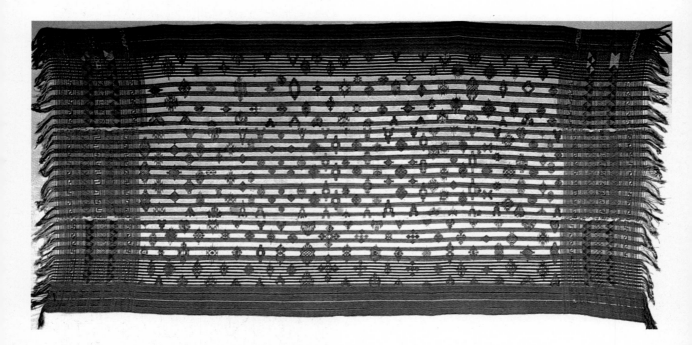

43. Detail showing interplay between stripes and Buddhist symbols.

44. Very old, worn *kushutara* with free-flowing, very traditional design. The raw silk Borders have holes where old style spike-type fibulas were used to hold the dress together at the shoulders. Could be mid-19th century or older. 272 x 135.

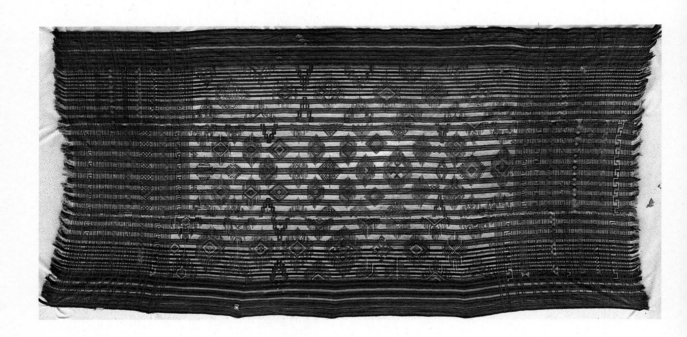

45.   Detail showing exhuberance of work.

46. Classic, beautiful antique *kushutara* with large, almost alphabet-like, designs. 19th century. 225 x 137.

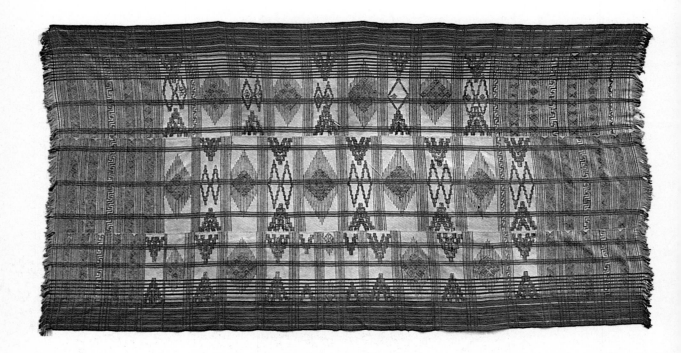

47. Centre diamond detail.   48. Detail from the border area.

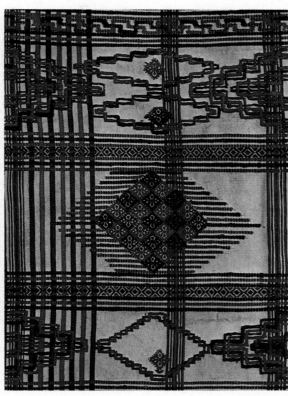

49. A simple, elegant *kushutara* with large brocaded designs in vibrant red and blue vegetable dye; silk-like quality in the texture of the background cotton. Probably from the turn of this century. 265 x 130.

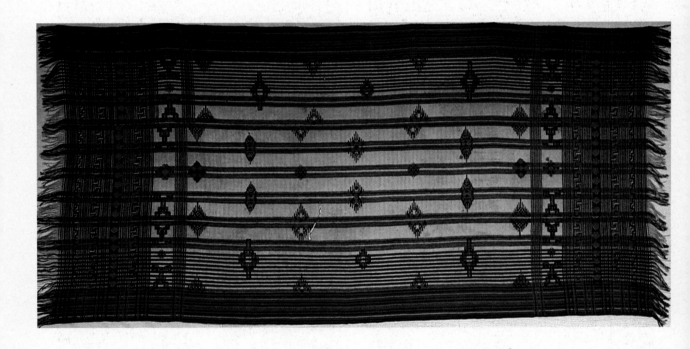

50. A rare *kira* of blue background and sides, with a white center panel. Well made with mainly aniline dyes. 255 x 142.

58

51. Beautiful *shibui* classic, antique *kushut-ara:* Perfectly matched and finished warm light blue and red. 19th century or older. 270 x 137.

52. Perfect craftsmanship is seen in this border detail.

53. Dazzling unique piece with use of brilliant vegetable dyes on Bhutanese cotton. Bold use of unusual traditional designs. 19th century or older. 255 x 130.

54. Detail of small designs worked into central area.

55. Detail of blue side border with interesting triangular design.

E. *SECHU*

56. Unusual *kushutara:* The striped borders are pure *sechu* as is the decoration on the white cotton field. The yellow center stripes are of raw silk using the continuous weft, double-faced technique as in the *aikapur.* 30-40 years old. 245 x 130.

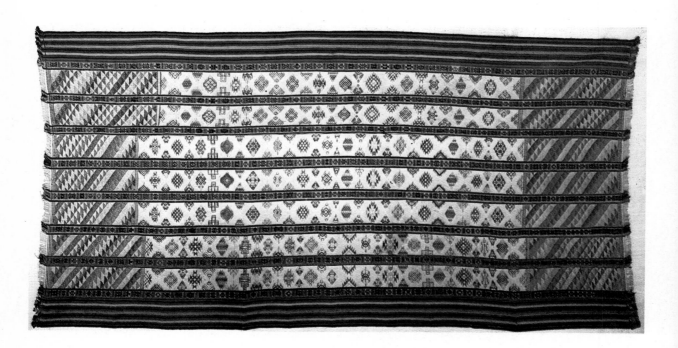

57. Two forms of weaving are seen in this detail.

58. Reverse side.

59. *Sechu* embellishment on medium to light cotton, mostly aniline dyes. The lightly embellished center spaces give visual relief from the crowded pattern when hung, and disppear into the fold of the kira when worn. The elongated diamond design is very popular in Bhutan. The areas around the design make patterns of their own when seen at night or from a distance. 20 to 30 years old. 255 x 140.

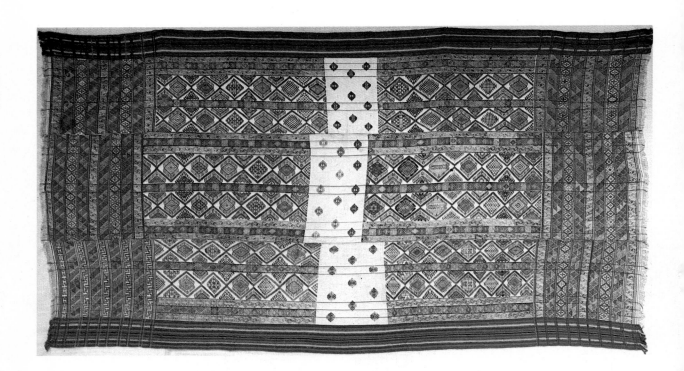

60. Portion of center panel with fine detail of *sechu* work.

61. Enlargement of plate 60.

62. Green, blue and maroon striped *jang-shem* decorated with fine *sechu* Buddhist symbols. Said to have been woven for the wife of an important Lama. 40-60 years old. 265 x 148.

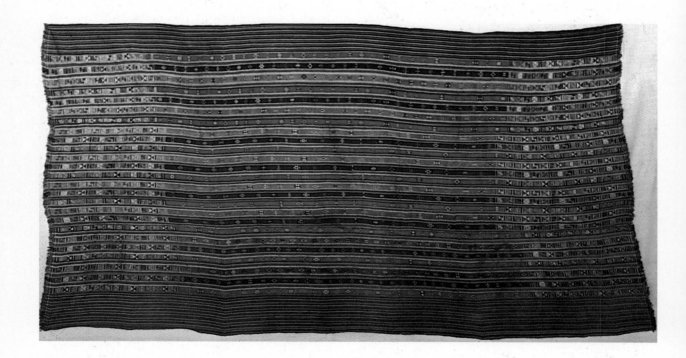

63.   Fine detail of the centre panels.   64.   Intricate work of an end border.

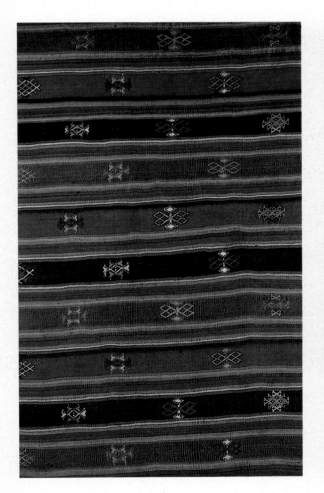

65. Solid, beautifully matched and spaced *kushutara*. Heavy cotton with glowing *sechu* embellishment. Every symbol is a masterpiece. 60-80 years old. 240 x 130.

66. Finely made symbols.

67. Fine workmanship provides a "cushion-like" effect to the individual diamonds within the symbols.

68. Green *jangshem* with alternating red and blue stripes. Dazzlingly fine *sechu* brocading. Interesting assymetrical spacing of design provides movement and visual variety rarely encountered in modern *kira*. About 20 Years old. 235 x 138.

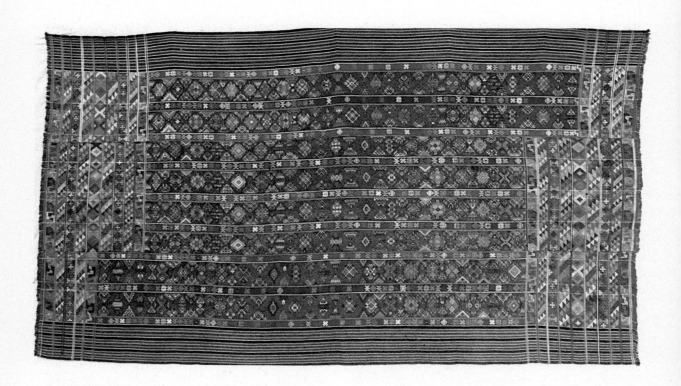

69. Detail showing intricacy of work.

70. Detail of minutely fine weaving on end border.

CHAPTER III

THE *KOH*

71. The traditional four long pieces needed to make a *koh*. *Lungsema* cloth — *buré on bure*.

72. Detail of *dromchu chaimo koh*, showing the finely embellished patterns of Tashigang.

73. Three lengths of *ada mata* cloth which will be used for the making of a *koh*.

Beautifully woven bamboo hat , which is worn in Bhutan as protection against sun and rain.

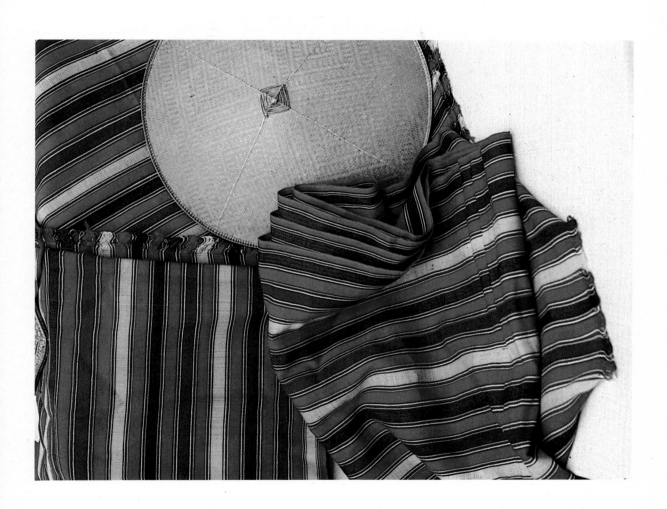

74. *Sechu* on *sechu koh* made from cloth called *dromchhu chaimo* in Tashigang where it was woven.

75. Beautiful *mentse mata koh*, yellow silk
embellishment upon red silk.

76. *Ada mata koh* with strong un-decorated striping.

77. *Lungsema koh* with raw silk brocading on raw silk.

CHAPTER IV

THE *KERA*

78. Vivid aniline dyed wool decoration on yellow cotton background. Unusually narrow for a *kera*. This one is shown as taken from the loom.   178 x 28.

79. Bright aniline dyed wool on a white cotton background.   The red dye has bled into the white background material and the fringe is oddly unfinished on one side. 138 x 33.

80. Black and red raw silk on white cotton. Discreet touches of color in narrow strips. Balanced spacing of woven stripes on upper white portion, although when worn this part is not seen. 40-50 years old. 160 x 35.

81. Detail of the white cotton portion with silk embrordery, which is not seen when worn.
↓

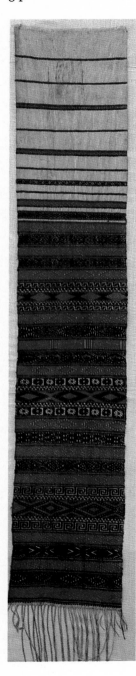

← 82. Finely woven classic black and red *kera* with elaborate embroidery. 30-40 years old. 200 x 35.

83. Detail of central portion.

84. Very fine soft *kera*. Black and red raw →
silk on cotton with some discreet touches of
colour. 175 x 32.

85. Section of the fringe end showing the
fine workmanship.

← 86. Classic blue and red vegetable dye *buré* embellished *kera*, on heavy unbleached cotton. Probably 19th century. 208 x 38.

87. This central detail brings into closer view the 'old-style' embellishment.

88. Another detail of this fine, traditional
kera.

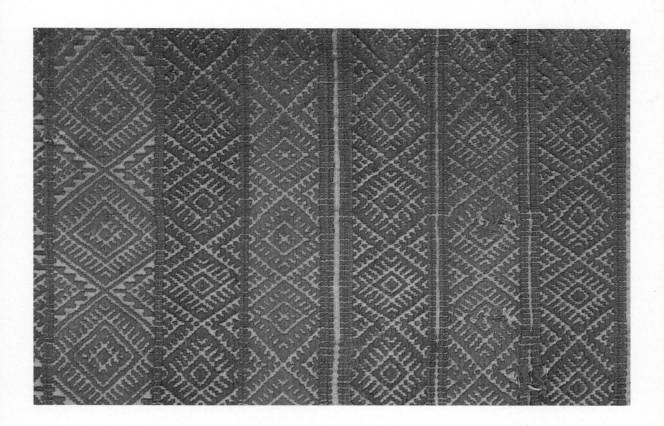

← 89. Shiny filament silk *(sechu)* embellishment on mustard yellow cotton. Probably woven to wear with one of the recent *sechu kushutara.*

90. Fine border detail from lower portion near fringe.

91. Central area detail.

92. An assortment of modern *kera*. The narrow striped one is used by the Bhutanese men for gathering the *koh* at the waist.

CHAPTER V

THE *KISHUNG*

A. *KISHUNG*

93. Nicely aged *shibui* poncho with swastikas on the shoulders and *torma* above the well-worn border. Criss-cross embroidery on the neck was probably added later. Early 19th century. 115 x 82.

94. Very fine, technically difficult, weaving of classic, nicely spaced decoration. Notice the swastikas: The ones on the right shoulder are Buddhist, whilst the ones on the left are *bon*. On the reverse side the swastikas move in the *bon* direction. Early 19th century or even earlier. 112 x 83.

← 95. Classic, unusually clean poncho: green and red *bure* embellished bleached cotton. Note the *torma* just over the border, and the stylized prayer boxes, or *gau,* on the shoulders. Probably turn of the century. 114 x 90.

96. Carpet—like lower border — a technique which has been lost since this poncho was made.

97. A very early *kishung* (poncho) woven from cotton with *jatsho* red and indigo blue raw silk embellishment. Note the simplicity and spacing of the design, especially on the bottom border, compared to later *kishung.* Possibly 18th century. The fringe and shoulder have been damaged in the course of time. Length 103 cm, width 85 cm.

98. A border detail showing the endless knot symbol.

← 99. Stunningly executed *kishung* in good condition. Embellished with *torma,* prayer wheels, *gau,* and beautiful original swastika-within-swastika design on the shoulders. The ribbon work at the neck has been added later. Probably mid-19th century. 123 x 88.

101. Detail of the fine weaving on both sides of the front center seam.

100. Right shoulder.

102. Early 19th century or perhaps earlier heavy cotton poncho with bold raw silk embellishment. The felt and ribbon work have been added later. 118 x 90.

103. *Gau* — amulet box design.

← 104. A stunning aristocratic poncho with flower field and swastika designs on the shoulders, a rare tree of life symbol below, ornate *torma* in center portion and intricately fashioned birds above a heavily embellished border. Late 19th century. 120 x 90.

↓ 105. Shoulder embellishment with tree of life symbol below.

106. Bird design from the left side. →

107. This charming, recent but spontaneous poncho was represented to me as Bhutanese, but it may have come from Tawang or one of the villages near the border between Bhutan and Arunachal Pradesh in India. The background cloth called *eu* is made from the stinging nettle plant, called *soucha*. 123 x 84.

108. Reverse side detail.

B.   *LAUSHINKA*

109. This type of poncho is called *laushinka* by the Bhutanese. This particular one, of heavy handwoven maroon wool has been adorned at the neck and sides by wool appliques and framed with intricately worked ribbons. Probably from the border area between tashigang and Tawang. 118 x 80.

110. Neck detail.

111. Charming animal detail from a side panel.

C. *NAUSHINKA*

112. *Naushinka* is the name of this blue wool poncho. *Nau* means blue and *lau* red in the Bhutanese language. Small pieces of chinese brocade have been appliqued onto dark blue wool and then framed with intricately worked ribbons.

113. Neck detail.

114. Beautiful applique from a side panel.

CHAPTER VI

THE *CHAKSEY PANGKEP*

A. *CHAKSEY PANGKEP*

← 115. Recent *chaksey pangkep.* Nice *sechu*
← work including lightning on the borders; in
← aniline dyes on yellow cotton. 210 x 73.

← 116. *Sechu* aniline dye embellishment on
← black cotton, a recent and rather jarring
← piece, but expertly executed. 20-30 years
old. 206 x 83.

← 117. Another unusual *chaksey pangkep* em-
← bellished on black; Orange, mauve, green and
white raw silk embellishment on rather light
cotton. Perhaps 30-40 years old. 213 x 95.

← 118. Classic well spaced elegant *chaksey
pangkep.* Multiple diamond design in the
center, and double rows of lightning run-
ning the entire length of both borders. Probably 19th century. 240 x 88.

119. Vibrant *jatsho* red and indigo blue
embellishment with four rows of lightning
on the borders make this an interesting piece.
Some damage has occurred to this 19th century piece. 245 x 85.

120. Border detail.   121. Detail of central area.

122. An elegant *chaksey pangkep* with →
classic blue and red vegetable dye brocading.
Unusually delicate work on the borders.
Slightly damaged due to age as probably made
during the 19th century. 154 x 98.

123.   The fine border work.
↓

124.   This detail of the centre shows intricate and delicate workmanship.
↓ ↓

← 125. *Jatsho* red raw silk with blue, yellow and white rough *bure* embellishment. Turn of the century or later. 235 x 70.

126. Pleasantly executed centre diamond. ↓

127. *Shibui jatsho chaksey pangkep* using lovely soft vegetable colours and traditional designs, including ligtnining on the borders. Feels like gossamer to the touch. 19th century. 254 x 78.

128. Lower center panel.

129. Very fine and rare *chaksey pangkep* with glowing multi-color *sechu* embellishment on *jatsho* red raw silk background. An unusual design is seen at the fringed ends with include ornate birds. 245 x 83.

130. A section of the center with parallel side borders.

131. The bird design which probably represents a peacock.

B.   *PANGKEP*

← 132. *Pangkep.*   Unusual burnt orange fine
← raw silk embellishment on bleached cotton.
← 40—50 years old. 205 x 68.

← 133.   Vibrant indigo blue and *jatsho* red raw
← silk embellishment on heavy unbleached
Bhutanese cotton.   Perhaps 19th century.
235 x 65.

← 134. *Pangkep.*   Vegetable and aniline dyed
raw silk embellishment on heavy white cotton. 20-30 years old. Regretably the corners
have been damaged. 208 x 70.

135.   Fine work on the center panel.

136. Finely embellished and spaced *buré* work on almost invisibly striped cotton. Small symbols spaced on the side borders. Slightly damaged. 70-80 years old. 268 x 78.

137. Symbols carefully spaced on the side border.

138. Somewhat simple *buré* embellishment on heavy *jatsho* red raw silk. Difficult to determine the age, but probably made at the turn of the century. 210 x 72.

C. *CHUKEP*

139. Very powerful *chaksey pangkep*, probably of the type known as *chukep*. Vivid blue and red raw silk embellishment on *neringma* cotton. Emphatically adorned with swastikas, lightning and thunderbolt symbols. A unique piece, perhaps 50—70 years old. 250 x 75.

140. Center diamond with supporting side borders.

↓

141. Outer border.   →

CHAPTER VII

YATA

A. *DENGKEP*

142. Long *yata* strip, woven to become a *dengkep*. Seen here as it has been removed from the loom. It will be cut across the middle, the fringes tied off, and sewn to become a carpet piece similar to the following pieces. 310 x 50.

143. Busy, aniline-dye embellished *yata* carpet piece, hemmed but not bound. 155 x 98. →

144. Detail.
↓

145. White wool carpet piece embellished with blue, red and yellow wool. A nice movement is seen in the flower pattern. 155 x 85.

146. Detail of plate 145.

147. *Dengkep.* Unusually large old-style rug or bed-cover. Vegetable dyed wool has been brushed after weaving. Bound with light blue twill. 194 x 109.

148. Detail of center.

149. More recent, unusually matched carpet piece attempting a carpet-like border design. Mixed aniline and vegetable colours. 145 x 84.

150. Detail of plate 149.

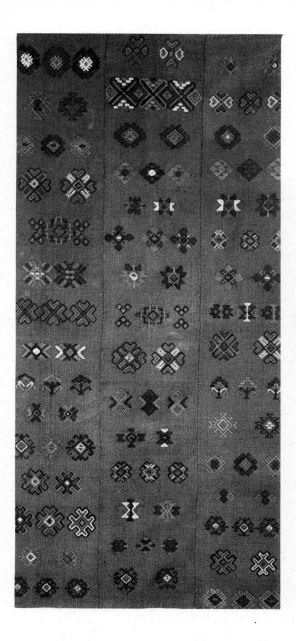

151. Small modern carpet on turquoise wool with aniline dyes. 150 x 73.

152. Detail of plate 151.

B. *CHARKEP*

153. *Charkep.* Three strips of *yata* cloth sewn together and bound at the edges with maroon twill, originally used as a raincoat or protection against cold weather. The beautifully elongated diamond in the center indicates that it was made for an important person. Note the tree of life design at the top of the center panel and the use of soft vegetable colors. This is an antique piece. 128 x 118.

154. Another antique *charkep* blanket piece. Vegetable colour, brushed wool embellishment on twill-like wool with huge diamond design in the center. 125 x 133.

155. A more recent *charkep* with gold
brocade, which may indicate that it belonged
to an important person, although it lacks the
large central diamond design. Pleasant tree
of life design in upper left hand corner.
138 x 118.

156. Bright, typical three-strip *charkep* on orange and white striped wool. Bound with light blue twill. 128 x 98.

CHAPTER VIII

CEREMONIAL SCARVES

A. *RACCHU*

157. *Racchu.* Brand new scarf made of rayon and worn by women when entering the Dzong This may be a replica of an older piece.

158. Recent *racchu* — Mixed cotton and rayon background with cotton embellishment at the fringed ends and with slight touches of lurex thread. Thread colour change on one side. 212 x 42.

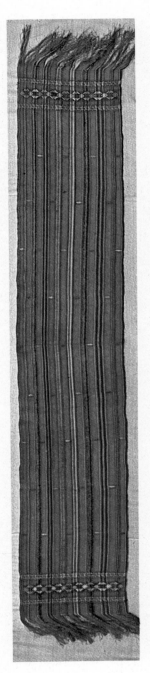

← 159. Antique *racchu* with bold *bure* embellishment on *jatso bure* background. Said to be called *ada racchu* and held in high esteem in Bhutan.

160. Pure *sechu racchu* with *sechu* brocading.

← 161. *Racchu* embellished overall. This is an old-style scarf worn by women on ceremonial occasions and sometimes used to carry a baby on their backs. Nice multi-coloured traditional embellishment on heavy cotton. 235 x 43.

162. Detail of plate 161.

163. Old, pure *sechu* scarf with lovely stripes →
and heavy embellishment at the fringed ends.
Badly stained, and the red dye has run in
washing. The Bhutanese say that two such
scarves are joined horisontally and worn by
sorcerers during healing sessions: 30-40
years old. 250 x 48.

164. Detail of the border at one fringed end.

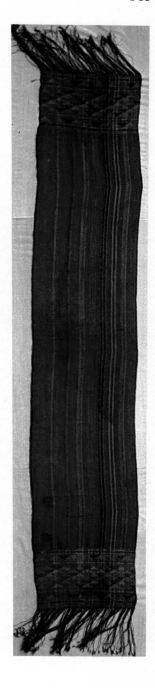

B.   *KUPNEY*

165. Group of Bhutanese wearing scarves.

166. This type of *kupney* or man's ceremonial scarf is known as *khamar* and is worn by certain high officials . The *khamar* is always white bordered by maroon. A new piece. 234 x 78.

CHAPTER IX

MISCELLANEOUS TEXTILES

167. Carry bag called a *pechu*. Used for carrying lighter objects on the back. This piece has black and red decoration on thick white cotton. Lengths of brown wool and cotton are used to attach the straps. This traditional carry bag is woven in a long strip then cut into two, joined and finished. 58 x 60.

168. Portion of the long, red, beautifully woven, piece shown in plate 167 used to make a carry bag. Intricate embellishment on red cotton background. 265 x 30.

169. A *bhindi* or carry bag. Black and red embellishment on simple white cotton. Ropes on the diagonal sides (corners) of this piece are tied together to carry bedding and other heavy loads. 126 x 126.

170-172.   Details of pate 169.

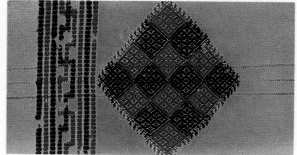

173. Very early woven piece which may have been used as a seat cover or hung behind a Lama or used as a carpet. It has been woven in vegetable coloured raw silk on old fine cotton in three narrow strips, using old Designs and supplementary weft technique and placed together to form a perfect rectangle with swastikas in the center. Framed in blue cotton twill and red felt, fringed and backed with khaki cotton twill. Very damaged, expecially the center swastika, but very beautiful and rare.

174. Detail of one corner.

175. This multi-colored *mandala*-like applique piece is fringed on all four sides bordered
with red and green wool felt and backed
with raw silk. It is an antique piece with
some damage. 150 x 140.

176. This square appliqué piece was said to have covered the saddle of the horse of a nobleman, to indicate his stature and rank. Central *yin yang* surrounded by wonderfully stylized snow lions. 96 x 101.

177. Detail of central *yin yang* symbol of plate 176.

178. Beautiful 19th century appliqué piece with central *yin yang* design, bordered on four sides by cheerfully striding phoenix. This piece was represented to have been hung over the outstretched arm of the retainer accompanying a nobleman. It could also have been used as an altar cloth. 155 x 70.

179. Close-up of one of the birds showing the artistry and imagination of the Bhutanese craftsmen.

180. This beautiful woolen fringed appliqué piece was probably used by a Lama as an altar cloth, or to keep ritual and religious objects on. Blue and yellow applique on a red background includes a center *chakra*. 90 x 60.

181. *Chakra* or eight-spoked wheel design.

182. A double bag with delightful appliqué used by a person of importance for carrying food while travelling. 187 x 43 (pair).

183. Another appliqué piece of similar vintage as plate 182. Said to be cover for drum used to announce the arrival of an important person when entering a town or village. 85 x 95.

184. Close-up of snow lion from plate 176.
Bhutan is traditionally known as "the land of
the thunder dragon". Could it not equally
be called "the land of the smiling snow-
lion"?